GW01376481

First published in 2008
Second printing 2009

Published by
Affirmations Australia Pty Ltd
34 Hyde Street, Bellingen NSW 2454 Australia
t: +61 2 6655 2350
e: sales@affirmations.com.au
www.affirmations.com.au

Designed and Edited by
Suzanne and Barbara Maher

10 9 8 7 6 5 4 3 2

ISBN 978-0-9805377-1-0

Printed in China on recycled paper using vegetable based inks.

jewels

Whatever you can do or dream you can do, BEGIN IT.

JOHANN VON GOETHE

Every new beginning comes from some other beginnings end.

listen to
ntuition

Listen to your intuition,
it will tell you
everything
you need to know.

When a great moment
knocks on the door of your life,
very often it's no louder
than the beating
of your heart.

BORIS PASTERNAK

Renew yourself
completely each day,
do it again and again,
and forever again.

CHINESE INSCRIPTION

Share your inspiration
with others.

ROBERT LOUIS STEVENSON

Small opportunities
are often the beginning
of great enterprises.

DEMOSTHENES

On life's journey
faith is nourishment,
virtuous deeds are a shelter,
wisdom is the light by day
and right mindfulness
is the protection by night.
If you live a pure life,
nothing can harm you.

BUDDHA

Enthusiasm is the greatest asset in the world.

HENRY CHESTER

Live in order
to fulfull
your potential.

RALPH WALDO EMERSON

Let the world know you
as you are,
not as you think
you should be.

FANNY BRICE

live for today

Life is a gift
we're given each day.
Dream about tomorrow
but live for today.

Remember that
what you have now
was once among the things
you only hoped for.

EPICURUS

It is possible
to move a mountain
by carrying away small stones.

CHINESE PROVERB

The most important
kind of freedom
is to be who you really are.

Do the best you can,
where you are,
with what you have,
now.

AFRICAN-AMERICAN PROVERB

Originality
does not consist
in saying what no one
has ever said before,
but in saying
exactly what you think
yourself.

faith in yourself

What you *get*
by achieving your goals
is as important
as what you *become*
by achieving your goals.

KAHLIL GIBRAN

Live with integrity,
respect the rights
of other people,
follow your own bliss.

NATHANIEL BRANDON

Take every opportunity
that is offered in your life,
it may never be offered again.

own bliss

If you are
a master of one thing
and understand one thing well,
you have at the same time,
insight into and
understanding of
many things.

VINCENT VAN GOGH

Let your heart guide you.

Know how to give
without hesitation,
and how to lose
without regret.

GEORGE SAND

Never forget that
the most powerful force
on earth is love.

NELSON ROCKEFELLER

Love
as much as you can,
give all you have,
and always forgive.

Nothing is more noble,
nothing more honoured
than fidelity.
Faithfulness and truth
are the most sacred endowments
of the human heart.

MARCUS CICERO

When you reach the top,
keep climbing.

It doesn't matter
how slowly you go,
so long as you do not stop.

CONFUCIUS

ision
your mind

The vision that you
hold in your mind,
the ideal that you
enthrone in your heart,
this you will build your life by,
and this you will become.

JAMES LANE ALLEN

Keep love in your heart,
it brings a warmth
and richness to life
that nothing else can bring.

OSCAR WILDE

Now and then it's good
to pause in our
pursuit of happiness
and just be happy.

GUILLAUME APOLLINAIRE

Think of what
a precious privilege it is
to be alive, to breathe, to think,
to enjoy, to love.

MARCUS AURELIUS

We know what we are,
but know not
what we may be.

The human heart
has hidden treasures.
The thoughts, the hopes,
the dreams, the pleasures.

CHARLOTTE BRONTE

Destiny is not
a matter of chance,
it is a matter of choice;
it is not a thing
to be waited for,
it is a thing to be achieved.

WILLIAM JENNINGS BRYAN

bring happ

To enjoy good health,
to bring true happiness
to your family,
to bring peace to all,
you must first discipline
and control your own mind.

If you can
control your mind
you can find
the way to
Enlightenment,
and all wisdom
and virtue
will naturally
come to you.

BUDDHA

Love is all we have,
the only way that each
can help the other.

EURIPIDES

All that I can,
I will.

FRENCH SAYING

Today, see if you can
stretch your heart
and expand your love
so that it touches
not only those to whom
you can give it easily,
but also to those
who need it so much.

At the centre
of your being
you have the answer;
you know who you are
and you know
what you want.

LAO TZU

Allow the beauty
of your soul to shine.

Dream
what you want to dream,
go where you want to go
and be who you want to be.

Enjoy the little things in life,
for one day
you may look back
and realise
they were the big things.

Accept your life
just as it is.
Today. Now.

Manifest plainness,
embrace simplicity,
reduce selfishness,
have few desires.

LAO TZU

hings

Every person
has an inborn worth
and can contribute
to the human community.
We all can treat one another
with dignity and respect,
and help one another
discover and develop
our unique gifts.

your
mind open

Have a heart
that never hardens
and a touch
that never hurts.

Live in the present
and make is so beautiful
it will be worth remembering.

BUDDHIST SAYING

Be thankful
for everything
that happens to you.

be thankful

A generous heart,
kind speech
and a life of service
and compassion
are the things
which renew humanity.

BUDDHA

Minds are like
parachutes:
They only function
when open.

THOMAS DEWAR

Love is infectious and
the greatest healing energy.

SAI BABA

The secret of health
for both mind and body
is to live
in the present moment
wisely and earnestly.

BUDDHA

You are today
where your thoughts
have brought you;
you will be tomorrow
where your thoughts take you.

JAMES LANE ALLEN

Life is just a path.
If you follow your heart
it will lead you
in the right direction.

The love we give away
is the only love we keep.

ELBERT HUBBARD

When you believe
in the impossible,
it becomes possible.

Passion makes all things
alive and significant.

RALPH WALDO EMERSON

The best things in life
are truly unseen,
that is why we close our eyes
when we kiss
and when we dream.

Reflect upon your present blessings, of which everyone has plenty.

CHARLES DICKENS

Be like a postage stamp. Stick to one thing until you get there.

JOSH BILLINGS

Life in abundance
comes through great love.

ELBERT HUBBARD

are blessed

Always be on the lookout
for ways to nurture
your dreams.

LAO TZU

Be content
with what you have,
rejoice in the way things are.
When you realise
there is nothing lacking,
the whole world
belongs to you.

LAO TZU

Move forward
with optimism and growth,
and realise the future
with hope, courage
and determination.

our dreams

If you are content
to simply be yourself
and don't compare or compete,
everybody will respect you.

LAO TZU

If you know
what you want out of life
it's amazing how opportunities
will come to enable you
to carry them out.

JOHN GODDARD

When you let go
of what you are
you become
what you might be.

The most effective way
to achieve right relations
with any living thing
is to look for the best in it.

It makes absolutely
no difference whatsoever
what people think of you.

RUMI

The biggest room
in the world
is the room
for improvement.

Nurture your mind
with great thoughts.

BENJAMIN DISREALI

If we go down
deep inside ourselves
we find that we possess
exactly what we desire.

SIMONE WEIL

your mind

Let us not be content
to wait and see
what will happen,
but rather make
the right things happen.

HORACE MANN

The will to win,
the desire to succeed,
the urge to reach your
full potential...
these are the keys
that will unlock the door
to personal excellence.

CONFUCIUS

Everyone has inside of them
a piece of good news.
The good news is
that you don't know how
great you can be,
how much you can love,
what you can accomplish,
and what your potential is.

great
can you be?

Titles in this series:

angels

ISBN 978-0-9804060-6-1

bliss

ISBN 978-0-9804060-7-8

friendship

ISBN 978-0-9804060-8-5

illumination

ISBN 978-0-9804060-9-2

inspiration

ISBN 978-0-9805377-0-3

jewels

ISBN 978-0-9805377-1-0